ڤنچارن قيصه نبي٢ عليهم السّلام

Musa

Abdul Rahman Rukaini

MACMILLAN PUBLISHERS

Bahasa Malay edition first published 1984.
Published by Macmillan Publishers (M) Sdn. Bhd. co-publication with Pustaka Pertubuhan Kebajikan Islam Malaysia.

This edition first published 1985

Published by *Macmillan Publishers Ltd*
London and Basingstoke
Associated companies and representatives in Accra, Auckland, Delhi, Dublin, Gaborone, Hamburg, Harare, Hong Kong, Kuala Lumpur, Lagos, Manzini, Melbourne, Mexico City, Nairobi, New York, Singapore, Tokyo.

ISBN 0–333–41421–7 (cased)
ISBN 0–333–40019–4 (pbk)
Printed in Hong Kong

Adviser for text:
Ustaz Haji Abu Hassan Din al-Hafiz

Adviser for illustrations:
Abdul Aziz Ibrahim

Designer and artist:
Abdul Razak Abdullah.
(ERAL)

Illustrations found in these series were not meant to depict all the prophets, their companions, or anyone concerned during that time. These illustrations were only meant to picture the situation or episodes that happened during that time. The Publisher has consulted authorised personnel to seek their advice regarding the contents and illustrations.

British Library Cataloguing in Publication Data
Rukaini, Abdul Rahman
Stories of the prophets of Islam.
1. Prophets in the Koran—Biography—Juvenile literature
I. Title
297'.122'0922 BP134.P745

ISBN 0–333–41421–7 (cased)
ISBN 0–333–40019–4 (pbk)

Preface

This volume concerns the life of the prophet Musa; from the time when he was placed in a floating box on the Nile to the time when he confronts the cruel King of Egypt and the proud Qarun.

Women play an important part in these stories: Yukabad, the prophet Musa's mother, and Asiah, the King's wife, and Safura, the daughter of the prophet Syu'aib who became the wife of Musa.

There are others also who help the prophet Musa: the prophet Syu'aib, the prophet Harun and the prophet Khidir.

The power of Allah is shown in the parting of the Red Sea and in the earthquake that destroys Qarun.

These stories are carefully selected and creatively written to appeal to young readers.

Illustrations

Contents

بسم الله الرحمن الرحيم

The floating box

On the banks of the river Nile there stood a small house. Tall green trees grew around it, and a cool breeze blew from the river. But the woman who lived in the house was too frightened to go outside. Her name was Yukabad and she was an Israilite. She was expecting a baby.

All the Israilites in Egypt lived in fear, because of the words of the astrologers. They had told the King, 'A boy child of the tribe of Israil will be born and he will live in Egypt. He will oppose the King and defeat him. He will not accept the King as a god.'

The King was angry and ordered every Israilite boy child to be killed. Pregnant women were afraid to go outside in case the King's men saw them. They searched any house where a baby was born. If the baby was a boy, they would kill it.

Yukabad prayed she would have a girl. As the time came for her baby to be born she prayed to Allah that her child would be safe. Faith in Allah gave her strength.

At last, the child was born. It was a beautiful baby boy and they called him Musa. Yukabad and her family loved him but their joy at his birth was mixed with fear. His birth was a secret. Only the family in the little house by the Nile knew about it. Yukabad looked after her baby and kept him indoors. But sometimes her faith in Allah was shaken by her fear for the child. One day the King's men came to the little house. Yukabad managed to hide the baby just in time but now she was more frightened than ever.

'What will I do if they come again?' she wondered. At night, when she closed her eyes, she saw her child's blood spilled on the ground as he cried out for the last time. Her fear was unbearable. But Allah understood the fears of the people in that little house. He sent Yukabad a dream, to show her what to do. Allah told her to prepare a

little box and put the baby into the box. The box would float on the river and the baby would be safe.

Yukabad watched with tears in her eyes as the precious box floated down the Nile. She had faith in Allah but her heart ached as the water took her baby away. She told her daughter to follow the box along the banks of the river.

The river flowed slowly so it was not difficult for the girl to keep the box in sight. Then she saw some women by a small landing stage. One of them was the King's daughter. The poor girl hid in fear as she watched the princess take the box from the water. What could she do? She turned and ran back to the little house as fast as she could.

'Mother!' she cried. 'The princess has found the box!' As they sat crying together, Yukabad still prayed to Allah to protect her son.

بسم الله الرحمن الرحيم

In the King's palace

When the King's wife, Asiah, saw the baby the princess had found, she loved him and wanted to keep him. But she couldn't look after a small baby herself. The baby needed a nurse. Yukabad went to the palace and offered herself for the job. Asiah agreed. She did not know that Yukabad was the baby's real mother.

Yukabad was so happy. She was allowed to take the baby home with her sometimes. As she walked back to the palace, along the road beside the great river, she looked at the clear water and thought of the little box that had floated on it. She held Musa close to her.

'May Allah protect you, my child', she said, and the baby smiled as if he understood.

Yukabad hated taking him back to the palace but she knew Asiah loved the baby very much. It was thanks to her that the King had not killed the child.

Asiah was always delighted to see the baby and his nurse. She took him from Yukabad and hugged and kissed him as if he were her own child. Yukabad had to smile as she watched Asiah play with him. She was glad Musa was safe, but she did not like him being with people who hated Allah and the people of Israil. These worries, though, she had to hide. She kept her mother's feelings secret in her heart.

When the King came in, he, too, smiled at the baby. He did not think this little child could harm him. He took the baby from Asiah's arms and began to play with him. But as the

King threw him up and caught him, Musa stopped laughing. Yukabad was afraid the change in the child would make the King angry and he would suspect something. She left quickly, in case she showed her fear. As she walked home along the river

bank, she prayed for the safety of her child.

The King tried to make the baby laugh again. He playfully pinched his cheeks but the child refused to smile. He stared coldly at the King, then his little hand took hold of the King's beard and pulled so hard that the King yelled in pain.

The King was furious. He threw the child to the floor. 'This must be

the child the astrologers told me about', he cried.

Asiah picked the boy up quickly.

'My dear, he's only a baby', she said as she held the child gently. She knew she had to be careful when the King was in a temper.

'Let go of that child!' shouted the King, but Asiah would not put the baby down. She loved Musa and did not want him to be hurt.

The King was furious and called for his palace guards. He ordered them to take the child away and kill him.

Asiah was horrified. With tears in her eyes she turned to her husband.

'Think of what you're doing', she said. 'He's only a baby. He didn't mean to hurt you. He doesn't understand what he's doing.'

The King stroked his beard thoughtfully.

'If you don't believe me, let us test him', said Asiah, still holding Musa.

'What do you mean?' said the King.

'We'll put a box of jewels and a box of hot coals in front of him. If he chooses the jewels, we will know he understands what he does and he will be killed. But if he takes the coals, that will be a sign that he is innocent', explained Asiah.

The King agreed and the boxes were put on the floor. As the baby crawled towards them, Asiah's heart beat faster. As he reached out towards the jewels she could not bear to look. But the angel Jibril was watching, and he turned Musa's hand to the hot coals. They turned cold as he picked them up.

The King smiled and said, 'The child knows nothing. He pulled my beard by mistake.' With a sigh of relief Asiah picked up the child and hugged him.

بسم الله الرحمن الرحيم

Musa arrives in Madyan

For eight days and eight nights Musa walked across the Sinai desert. At last Egypt was far behind him. Exhausted by his journey, he sat in the shade of a rock near the Gulf of Aqabah to rest.

He tried not to think of his thirst, or of the pain of his aching feet. He tried not to think, too, of his reason for escaping from Egypt. But as he closed his eyes, the face of the man he had killed rose again before him. He covered his face with his hands and his tears fell. He had not meant to hurt anyone. He had tried to stop a fight between an Israilite and one of the people of Egypt. The Israilites

were treated with such cruelty, and Musa could not bear to watch. He had to help the man. But he had not meant to kill his opponent. Musa knelt to ask Allah's forgiveness.

In the distance there were trees and flocks of goats. Musa saw a group of men standing round a well nearby. Two little girls stood to one side. They looked worried, so Musa went to help them.

'What's wrong?' he asked kindly.

'We have come to fetch water,' the girls replied shyly, 'but we are frightened of those men.'

'I'll get it for you', said Musa, although he was so tired from his journey. The girls thanked him and set off home with their water. When they got to their house, they told their father of the kindness of the man they had met at the well. The old man wanted to reward the person who had helped his daughters, so he sent them back to find him and invite him home.

The last rays of the setting sun were fading from the sky when they found Musa resting by the rock. Musa thanked them for their invitation and accepted. He felt it was a sign from Allah. He walked back with them to the house of their father, the prophet Syu'aib, who was to become Musa's father-in-law.

بسم الله الرحمن الرحيم

The burning bush

For ten years Musa had lived in the beautiful country of Madyan. He had married Safura, daughter of the prophet Syu'aib. His happiness had helped him forget his suffering as he crossed the Sinai desert all those years ago. But he could not forget his people in Egypt. He had promised the prophet Syu'aib he would stay for ten years, and now the time was up. He knew he had to return to Egypt to free his people from their slavery to the cruel King.

He told his wife, Safura, about his decision and spoke to his father-in-law. They were wise and did not try to stop him going.

Musa and his wife left the prophet Syu'aib's house with his blessing. They took food with them for the long and difficult journey.

Long after leaving the peaceful green valley of Madyan, they came to the foot of Mount Sinai. There was something special about this place. The air seemed different, there was silence all around. It seemed to Musa and his wife that

the spirit and greatness of Allah was in the mountain.

They had stopped because they were not sure of the way. It was evening and the heat of the sun was fading fast. A soft breeze began to blow and the shadows lengthened. Musa and his wife felt frightened as it got dark. They had no choice but to stop and camp for the night.

Musa told his wife they must put their trust in Allah. Allah made day and night. He would protect them now, and in the morning, when the sun spread its rays over the empty land, Allah would show them the way to Egypt.

They sat in silence for a while, watching the stars glittering in the sky. Suddenly they noticed a bright light in the valley. It wasn't a star, but the light of a fire.

'Safura, stay here', said Musa. 'I will go and get some fire, so we can build a fire here to warm ourselves.'

Safura agreed and watched as Musa walked carefully down the steep side of the valley. Once or twice he almost fell, but at last he reached a huge olive tree that grew near where the fire was. As he went on, he began to feel very frightened. Suddenly he wanted nothing more than to turn round and go back to his wife. He stopped for a moment to calm himself. Then he heard a voice.

'Musa, I am your Lord. Take off your shoes. You are walking on holy ground. I have chosen you as My prophet. Listen carefully. This is My message for you.' (*Al Quran, Surah Thaha, verses 12–13*)

This was Allah's first sign to the prophet Musa that He had chosen him to spread the faith of Islam.

Musa hurriedly took off his shoes. He was speechless as he knelt to listen to Allah's message.

'I am Allah. There is no other God but Me. Bow before Me and worship Me. I tell you that the Day of Judgement will come, but you will not know when it is to be. On that day, each man will be treated as he deserves. Do not let evil men persuade you to do wrong things. Do not listen to those who will not believe you.' (*Al Quran, Surah Thaha, verses 14–16*).

Allah told Musa that he must go back to Egypt and face the King.

Musa had a difficult task to carry out. He prayed to Allah, 'My God, make my task easier! Tell me what words to say so the people will listen to me. Let a member of my family, my brother Harun, help me . . .' (*Al Quran, Surah Thaha, verses 25–30*)

Allah understood how Musa felt. He knew Musa felt too weak to be able to carry out this great task.

Allah said to him, 'What is that you have in your hand, Musa?'

'It is my staff', the prophet answered.

Allah said, 'Throw it down!'

Musa did as Allah said, and to his astonishment, the staff changed into a huge snake. Musa was frightened and backed away.

Allah told him not to be afraid. He told him to walk up to the snake and pick it up. Musa did so, and as soon as he touched it, the snake became a staff again. Musa was no longer afraid. (*Al Quran, Surah Thaha, verses 17–21*)

The miraculous staff was Allah's gift to the prophet Musa. With the staff, Musa could face the cruel King.

Then the voice of Allah told the prophet to press his hands together. When he parted them again, they glowed with light. This was a sign that Allah would protect him.

Now Musa was no longer afraid of his task. He knew he could face the King of Egypt, because Allah was with him.

'Take my word to your people, with the prophet Harun', said the voice of Allah. 'You and your followers will triumph.' (*Al Quran, Surah Thaha, verse 42*)

With Allah's words still ringing in his ears, the prophet Musa went back to his waiting wife.

بسم الله الرحمن الرحيم

Musa meets the King

A splendid palace stood on the banks of the river Nile. It was enclosed by high stone walls and iron gates. Armed men stood on guard at the entrance. There were other guards at every door into the palace. Only important people were allowed into the palace.

This was where the King lived with his wife, Asiah, and their ministers and servants. This was also the palace where Musa had lived as a boy.

The King was a cruel ruler. From his palace he gave orders that made his people suffer. The children of Israil were treated worst of all. The King enjoyed his power. He was the ruler of the land but he also told the people he was their god, too. They must obey and worship him.

No one could get into the palace without permission. It was not easy to see the King. Anyone who wanted to, had to apply to his ministers first. Then he had to wait a long time while they decided whether to give him permission or not. Very few people wanted to see the King, though. The people were frightened of him. No one was brave enough to oppose him. Everyone hoped that one day someone would come along to help them, someone who was strong and brave and could stand up to the King. The King had ruled for a long time. How much longer could the people wait?

The two strangers waiting in the great hall did not seem to be afraid. They were not trembling, as most people did in the presence of the King. They did not bow to the King like everyone else.

'Who are you?' asked the King sharply. Every head turned towards the strangers.

The prophet Musa replied, 'We are Musa and Harun, the messengers of Allah who have been sent to you.'

The King looked puzzled. He did not understand.

'We want you to free the Israilites from their slavery under your cruel rule. We want you to set them free and let them worship Allah freely.'

The ministers gasped as they heard these words. Surely these men would be killed for speaking to the King like this! For a moment the King was speechless. No one had ever dared to speak to him like this before. Slowly, he rose from his throne. Then he pointed at Musa and said, 'Aren't you the Musa who lived in this palace as a child? We nursed you and looked after you!'

Musa replied calmly, 'Does that prove you are a good king? Doesn't it show your cruelty to the children of Israil? One child found safety in the palace but all the other boys were killed.'

Again the King was speechless for a moment. He had never met a man who answered a question with another question! He shook his head. 'So, Musa, you have forgotten our kindness to you.'

'I haven't,' replied the prophet, 'but there is no reason for you to be proud of looking after me in childhood. It only happened because of your cruelty. Because you ordered your men to kill every boy child, my mother had to put me in a box and float it down the Nile. Someone brought me from the river to your palace. I was saved from being killed by you.'

The King had not expected Musa to answer so calmly and clearly. He tried again. 'Did you not kill one of my people? Yet here you are, free and unpunished. Is that not a sign of our kindness to you?'

'That man's death was caused by one of the wicked people who try to make men slaves. But it has led to something good. When I was forced to run away from Egypt, Allah made me His messenger. I have come here as the messenger of Allah to beg you and your people to worship Allah, to forget your cruelty, to end the suffering of the children of Israil.'

The King went white with anger at the mention of Allah. The King would never let the people worship anyone but himself.

'Who is this God you speak of,

Musa? I am the god who is worshipped and praised in this world!'

This was just what Musa had wanted the King to say. Now he had the chance to show the listeners that the King was not really a god. He answered, 'Allah is your God and the God of your ancestors. He is God of the Earth and the sky, and the God of everything that is in the Earth and the sky.'

The ministers glanced at each other. It was clear they believed Musa. How could an ordinary man like the King be the god of all men?

The King was beginning to look worried. 'This messenger is mad!' he cried. The palace ministers were silent. They stood looking down at the ground. The King tried to argue with Musa again. He named all the people of the past who had worshipped idols, but Musa replied that these people had turned from the true path. Allah's guidance and wisdom had always existed. Those who chose to ignore it would be judged by Allah and would suffer for it.

The King could not accept defeat. 'Musa, if you believe in any god but me, I will have you thrown into prison!' he cried.

'Will you put me in prison if I can prove to you that I speak the truth?' asked the prophet.

The King hesitated, then reluctantly replied, 'Give me a sign.'

All eyes turned to the prophet.

بسم الله الرحمن الرحيم

The contest

Musa was ready to prove that he was the messenger of Allah. The proof would be sent from Allah, a special power given only to men like

Musa, the prophet Salih and the prophet Ibrahim.

The ministers and the palace magicians gathered round to watch. The King was sure the 'sign' would just be some childish trick.

'Very well,' he said scornfully, 'show me your proof. If you fail ...' he looked towards the armed guards.

Musa spoke the name of Allah. Then, with a quick prayer, he threw his staff to the floor. It changed into

a huge snake which slithered over the floor towards the King.

The King leapt up from his seat. He was speechless. His heart beat wildly and his body trembled. The snake came closer. The magicians tried their spells but they could not stop the snake. They watched the King in horror. The ministers scattered to save themselves. The palace guards ran here and there, trying to stab the snake with their spears, but their spears just fell from their hands.

In a trembling voice, the King begged Musa to call off his snake.

Calmly Musa picked up the snake. As he touched it, it became a lifeless staff once more. The King gave a sigh of relief. The ministers, magicians and guards relaxed once more.

Now the danger had passed, the King's pride returned.

'Musa,' he said, 'this proof is not enough. Can you show me nothing else?'

'Look at my hands', said Musa. When he took them from his pockets, they were shining with light. The King and his men were dazzled by the brightness.

But still the King would not admit that Musa and Harun were the messengers of Allah. He pointed accusingly at his ministers and magicians.

'You have seen the tricks of these madmen', he said. 'Do you accept defeat with their magic? Will you let them leave here in triumph?'

The men were still frightened of the King's anger. They had to think of something to save themselves.

One of them had an idea. 'Musa and Harun must be destroyed by their own magic', he said. 'There are many magicians in this country. We will hold a contest between them and Musa and Harun. Our magicians will defeat them.'

Everyone agreed. Musa smiled at Harun, telling him to have faith in Allah.

The contest was held the next day in a large field. The King and his ministers came to watch. Crowds of ordinary people came too.

The prophets spoke. 'You have sinned against Allah. You have dared to think His miracles were tricks. But you will be defeated. You will regret this day.'

The magicians had been promised a lot of money by the King. They all threw down sticks and bits of rope, which immediately turned into a mass of writhing snakes.

The crowd gasped in amazement. Then Musa threw his staff into the middle of the snakes. The staff turned into a huge snake. One by one, the magicians' snakes were swallowed by the prophet's. Not one was left.

The King went back to his palace with his men, with a face like thunder, but the magicians declared their faith in Allah and asked Him to forgive them for their sins.

بسم الله الرحمن الرحيم

Swallowed by the sea

The King had never been so angry. He did not know what to do. He walked up and down, sat down, stood up, held his head in his hands.

'It's your fault!' he shouted at his ministers and guards. They stood trembling before him. 'This man, Musa, and the Israilites—they were unarmed but you could not control them. You are not to be trusted!'

'Well, they went at night, Your Majesty', said one of the guards nervously.

'I don't care. You have let Musa and the Israilites make fools of you all. Why weren't you on guard at night?' snapped the King.

The guard was silent. It had become impossible to stop the prophet. Even in the palace there were people who supported him and followed his religion.

'I told you to watch Musa and the Israilites', said the King. 'But you have let them get away. Now you must search for them. We will punish anyone who tries to leave Egypt!'

'But where shall we search?' asked one of the guards.

'You fool!' shouted the King turning to the guard. He laughed as the guard trembled before him. 'So, you're afraid of me? Am I not your god?' The King laughed again. 'Only Musa and the Israilites do not call me god. We will find them. Bring horses and arrows and follow me!'

The King rode at the head of his ministers and well-armed soldiers. At the palace gates they lit their torches. The order was given, 'To the Red Sea!'

'To the Red Sea!' cried the soldiers as they rode off into the night. They had guessed that the prophet Musa and the people of Israil were on their way to Palestine.

The thunder of the horses' hooves broke the silence of the night as they rode across the desert. Only the flames of their torches could be seen in the cold darkness.

They rode for many hours. The horses were getting tired and slowed down. The torches were beginning to flicker and die out. Then, in the pale light of dawn, they saw a group of people standing on the shore of the Red Sea.

'There they are!' shouted the King. 'They can't escape now!'

The cries of the King's soldiers could be heard above the thunder of their horses' hooves. Some of the people on the shore were watching the vast rolling sea in front of them, others looked back at the advancing horses. Trapped between the King's men and the sea, the people began to panic. In danger of death, some of the prophet's followers turned against him. They were in despair. They could see no way of escape.

The hoof beats were nearer now. The hearts of the prophet's followers beat like the waves on the shore of the Red Sea. Had they suffered so much to come and die here?

'Musa, is this what you brought us here for? What will we do now? Behind us, our enemies are bearing down on us. Before us is the sea. We have no boats. How can we save ourselves?'

But the prophet remained calm. 'Do not be afraid', he said. 'Our journey has been blessed by Allah. Allah will show us the way to escape from our cruel enemies.'

But Musa's words were not enough to calm the people. Their faith was not strong enough.

So Allah ordered Musa to strike the waters of the Red Sea with his staff. The prophet obeyed. As his staff touched the water, the waves of the sea curled back. Dry land stretched out before them, making a pathway from the western to the eastern shore. On each side the water rose up like walls of crystal green.

The prophet and the children of Israil set out to cross the sea where the waters had divided.

The King and his men stopped for a moment in surprise. Then the King urged his men on.

'See my power', he lied. 'The Red Sea has divided in two so we can pass and kill Musa and the Israilites in the middle of the sea.'

The King and the armed soldiers rode on into the path through the sea. Suddenly there was a great roar. As the prophet Musa and the Israilites reached the eastern shore, the waters of the sea closed over the heads of the King and his men. All of them died under the waves.

As the King struggled in the water that cared nothing for his pride and power, he understood at last. 'I believe there is no God but Allah. The people of Israil worship Him and now I, too, worship Him.'

But it was too late. The King's lifeless body floated on the water. A pitiful end to the life of a cruel and arrogant king.

بسم الله الرحمن الرحيم

The wonderful cow

'There it is! There is the cow we are looking for!'

The people of the village were about to turn back, when at last they saw the cow. They had been looking for so long. They were going to go back and tell Musa they couldn't find the special cow he had asked for. Then they heard the cries of the men who had gone ahead,

'Here it is! We have found the cow!'

It was a very unusual cow. It was a golden colour and its skin seemed to glow. The people crowded round to admire it. 'Isn't it beautiful!' they cried.

Some people wondered who it belonged to, but most of them did not care. They only wanted to find out who had killed Syam'un bin Naftali, a wise and generous old man. Their voices and laughter rang out with excitement as they took the cow back to the village.

One man did not join in their celebration. This was Nadab bin Su'az. He grew pale as the cow came closer. One of his friends came running up to him. 'Nadab, here is the cow!' he said, smiling. 'Now the prophet Musa will be able to tell us who killed your uncle. When the murderer has been found and judged, you will be a rich man! You will inherit all your uncle's money—and you'll be able to marry Rufqah!'

Nadab said nothing. He smiled bitterly, but his friend did not notice anything was wrong and ran on.

Nadab sat alone under a tree. Now the truth would be known. He knew he had done wrong, but it was too late. He thought of all his sins. He was not a good man, like Ilyab bin Azar. He told lies and behaved badly. This was why his uncle had not accepted Nadab's proposal to marry Rufqah. Syam'un had chosen Ilyab, instead, to marry his daughter. When Syam'un was killed, Nadab had led the hunt for his murderer. Everyone agreed that if the search parties were unsuccessful, Nadab would inherit his uncle's wealth and marry Rufqah. Now Nadab knew the prophet Musa would find out the truth.

Another of his friends found him and took him along with the excited crowd to the field where Syam'un was buried. The whole village had gathered to see what would happen.

The cow was slaughtered according to the prophet Musa's instructions. Its tongue was cut out and given to Ilyab. The body of Syam'un had been dug up. Ilyab hit the dead body with the tongue of the cow. The corpse rose.

The prophet spoke. 'Tell us, Syam'un, who has murdered you.'

Syam'un's mouth opened and he said, 'The man who murdered me is Nadab, my own nephew.' With those words, the body fell lifeless to the ground again.

The people gasped. They had never suspected Nadab. Nadab had lied and fooled them all. The prophet Musa announced the punishment. Nadab must die. 'A life for a life!'

Nadab accepted the prophet's words in silence. His face was white. He stood alone, friendless.

Justice was done. Ilyab would marry Rufqah, the beautiful girl who had been the innocent cause of her cousin's crime, and Nadab would die.

بسم الله الرحمن الرحيم

You must not ask

The prophet Musa, as Allah's messenger, had seen much cruelty and suffering. He spent all his time trying to help people, teaching them to lead good lives and worship Allah. He tried to find out why people behaved badly and tried to change their ways. He questioned anything that was against his teaching. He spoke out against evil and cruelty. He fought against what was unfair and unjust in the world. He tried to understand why the world was as it was, and tried to make things better.

He wanted to learn from the prophet Khidir. Khidir had agreed to let the prophet Musa and his friend, Yusa' bin Nun, travel with him and learn from him. But before they set out, the prophet Khidir told them they must obey a strict rule.

'You must never ask anything while on a journey', Khidir told them. The prophet Musa and his friend promised to keep this rule.

But now the prophet Musa knelt before Khidir with a bowed head. He was ashamed. Three times he had broken the law of the journey. Three times he had questioned the prophet Khidir. He couldn't help it. He was so used to judging people's actions, to finding out what was right and what was wrong. He could not keep quiet when he saw something which was unjust or caused suffering. He had spoken out because the prophet's actions had seemed to be wrong.

'Why did you break the sides of that boat? Why did you kill that little child? Why did we build this embankment?' These were the questions he had asked Khidir.

The boat had been afloat. It belonged to some poor fishermen. Was it not wrong to destroy someone else's property? That was what Musa thought.

The prophet Khidir had wrung the neck of a small child. Was that not cruel? Musa had promised not to ask questions, but he could not keep silent!

The three travellers were sitting by the embankment they had just rebuilt. The people who lived in this place were greedy and selfish. Why had they rebuilt their embankment for them? Why not leave them unprotected and let them be destroyed?

Before they set out on their journey, the prophet Musa had said, 'I will try to be patient. I will try not to break the rule.' Now he was too ashamed to look at Khidir. Twice he had asked questions and then asked for the prophet's pardon. Now he was too ashamed to ask for pardon again. He knew he had done wrong.

He knew Khidir might tell him they could not travel together any more.

The prophet Khidir smiled as he looked at Musa. He knew why these actions had seemed wrong to Musa, but Khidir knew the reasons for them, too. He spoke gently to Musa.

'It is not possible for you to be patient. The time has come for us to part, Musa.'

Musa sat silently with his head bowed.

'Now I will tell you the meaning of those actions which troubled you and made you break your promise.'

Musa and his friend Yusa' listened quietly to the prophet Khidir's teaching.

'I damaged the fishing boat because the ruler of the country where the poor fishermen lived is a cruel man. He doesn't care about the poverty and suffering of his people. If he sees any good, strong boats he takes them for his own use. I broke the side of the boat so the King would not steal it. I did it to help the fishermen. They can still use their boat for fishing. I did not damage it badly.'

Musa and Yusa' began to understand.

'The child I killed was naughty and dangerous. His parents were good people, faithful to Allah. If the child had lived, he would have grown up and forced his parents to leave their faith. He would even have killed them. I did what I did to save the parents.'

'Now, the embankment. Allah has told me that this land is very valuable. The owner has left it for his two orphaned children. I repaired it so that in the future those childen will have valuable land. The people who live here now would let it be ruined.'

'I did all this because Allah gave me the knowledge. I was obeying the commands of Allah.'

The prophet Musa and the prophet Khidir now went their separate ways. As he made his way home, the prophet Musa remembered the story of the bird who thought he could empty the sea all on his own. The vast sea was like the wisdom of Allah and the knowledge of mankind as tiny as that bird! Musa knew how small his own knowledge was, even though he was the chosen messenger of Allah.

بسم الله الرحمن الرحيم

Qarun is destroyed

Qarun was richer than any other Israilite. He lived a life of luxury. He had worked for the old King of Egypt and now he was a close friend of the new King. This was how he had made so much money. He cared nothing about his own people, but helped the cruel ruler make them suffer. He travelled in Egypt and as far as Syria and Kan'an, using his influence to increase his own wealth. He would not listen to the teaching of Musa. He did not care about the suffering of others. He was rich, proud and selfish.

But now, for the first time, he was afraid. The prophet Musa had just been to see him. Qarun's face was white as he thought about the prophet's visit. The prophet had told Qarun he was cruel, greedy and proud, he had turned his back on his own people and was leading a wicked life. Qarun had no answer. He knew that everything the prophet said was true.

While the prophet was with him, Qarun had agreed to give his money to the poor, to help those who had nothing. The prophet was such a strong person, he spoke so well, that it was difficult not to believe him while he was talking to you. But now the prophet had gone, Qarun's feelings of pride and greed were coming back.

Qarun sat on his golden throne, thinking. He had promised to leave all his wealth to his family when he died. Why should the Israilites have it?

'No!' he said aloud. 'This throne, this palace, all my money belongs to me. I worked for it. The Israilites have not earned this wealth. I will not do as Musa asks. He is poor. He is just jealous of me. I will work against Musa. I have a lot of important friends who will help me.'

Qarun talked to one of his friends about the prophet Musa.

'This Musa is not a prophet', said Qarun. 'He's just a trouble-maker. He wants to take away the power of the rich people.'

'He's a magician', said Qarun's friend. 'He's got a lot of people under his spell. On my way here, I saw him talking to a large crowd of people in the town.'

'So a lot of people listen to him and believe in him?' asked Qarun.

'Oh yes', replied the friend, taking a sip of his wine.

'Then we must destroy him', Qarun decided. Qarun wanted to be the leader of the Israilites himself.

Qarun and his friend walked round the palace gardens so they could think in peace.

'It's no good just arguing with Musa', said Qarun.

'What are you going to do then?' asked his friend.

'That's what I'm trying to decide', said Qarun, walking up and down impatiently. Finally they decided to make up lies about Musa, among which they said that Musa had leprosy. That was why he was always wearing a long robe. They said too that the prophet Musa had killed the prophet Harun.

But all those slanders were proven lies by Allah. This was stated by Allah in the holy Quran.

'Do not be like those who have hurt Musa. Allah has cleared him of all those slanders. He is worthy in the eyes of Allah.' (*Al Quran, Surah al-Ahzab, verse 69*)

Qarun was defeated. That night his palace was shaken by an earthquake and as it fell in ruins Qarun was destroyed with all his riches.